Make a joyful noise to the Lord, all the earth! Serve the Lord with gladness! Come into his presence with singing! know that the Lord is God! It is he that made us and we are his; We are his people, and the sheep of his pasture. Ps. 100:1-3

ACKNOWLEDGMENTS. The editor and publisher have made every effort to trace the ownership of all copyrighted material and to secure permission from holders of the copyrights of such material. In the event of any question arising as to the use of any material, the editor and publisher, while expressing regret for inadvertent error, will be pleased to make the necessary corrections in future printings.

Basic Books, Inc., for "The Shema" and "A Jewish Prayer" ("Remember Us for Life"), from *Prayer in Judaism* by Bernard Martin, © 1968 by Basic Books, Inc., Publishers, New York.

Church Information Office, for "To You, O Lord, I Lift My Hands in Prayer," ("My Hand of Prayer"), from *God Is Looking After Me*, published by Church Information Office, Church House, Dean's Yard, London SW1P 3NZ.

Les Editions du Cerf, for "Grace," from *Table Prayer* by E. D. Bouyer.

Harper & Row, Publishers, Inc., for "A Japanese Prayer" ("For Quietness") by Utsomiya San, and for "Formosan Prayer" ("Grave Clothes Bind Me Still"), both from *The World at One in Prayer*, edited by Daniel Johnson Fleming. Copyright 1942 by Harper & Row. Also for "I am in every religion," from *The Choice Is Always Ours* by Dorothy B. Philips and Others. By permission of the publisher.

The Hebrew Publishing Company, for "A Child's Morning Prayer," "A Child's Evening Prayer," and "A Prayer for Hanukkah," from *The Jewish Woman and Her Home*, by Hyman S. Goldin.

Alfred A. Knopf, for "Heaven," from *Selected Poems* by Langston Hughes.

Macmillan Publishers Co., Inc., for "Little Things," from *Collected Poems* by James Stephens. Reprinted with permission of Macmillan Publishing Co., Inc.; of Mrs. Iris Wise, Macmillan London & Basingstoke; and of the Macmillan Company of Canada Limited. Copyright 1926 by Macmillan Publishing Co., Inc.; renewed 1954 by Cynthia Stephens.

Peter Pauper Press, for "Talking with one another," from African Proverbs by C. W. Laslau.

A. D. Peters and Company, for "Jesus Christ, Thou Child So Wise," from *Verses* by Hilaire Belloc. Reprinted by permission of the publisher.

Penguin Books Ltd., for "God of the winds and waters," from *The Bhagavad Gita*, translated by Juan Mascaro.

St. John's University Press, for "In dealing with others," from *Asian Institute Translations*, No. 1: Lao Tsu/Tao Teh Ching. Copyright 1961, St. John's University, New York.

Josephine Thecker, Administratrix of the Dixie Willson Estate, for "Dear God, I Gratefully Bow My Head," by Dixie Willson.

Union of American Hebrew Congregations, for "Grace After Meals," from *Within Thy Hands* by Ilo Orleans.

The Viking Press, Inc., for "The Prayer of the Mouse," "The Prayer of the Little Bird," "The Prayer of the Little Ducks," and "The Prayer of the Cricket," from *Prayers from the Ark* by Carmen Bernos de Gasztold (translated by Rumer Godden).

War Resisters League, for "An American Indian Prayer," from the 1974 WRL Peace Calendar, *As Long as the Rivers Shall Flow*.

E. P. Dutton & Co., Inc., for lines from *The Koran*, translated by Rev. J. M. Rodwell. Everyone's Library Edition. Reprinted by permission of E. P. Dutton & Co., Inc. and J. M. Dent & Sons, Ltd.

# The Golden Treasury of PRAYERS for Boys and Girls

Selected by Esther Wilkin

Illustrated by Eloise Wilkin

Golden Press • New York

Western Publishing Company, Inc.

Racine, Wisconsin

## Dedication

For Daniel, Brian, Mary Clare and Paul
David, Mark, John and Elizabeth
Amy and Sidney John
Michael, Chris, Patty, Kathy
Susan, Joan and Jamie

# FOREWORD

Some of our friends worship God in ways that are different from ours, for there are many ways of giving honor and glory to God, many ways of praying.

This book contains prayers that are new and prayers that are very old. They have been collected from all over the world and are used in worship by children everywhere.

When we pray, we lift our minds and hearts to God who loves us all. Let us all then be united with Him in love: the love of God for us, our love for Him, and our love for one another.

## Morning Prayer

Now before I run to play,
   Let me not forget to pray
To God who kept me through the night
   And waked me with the morning light.

Help me, Lord, to love Thee more
   Than I ever loved before,
In my work and in my play,
   Be Thou with me through the day.

                       Amen.

*Author Unknown*

For this new morning and its light,
For rest and shelter of the night,
For health and food, for love and friends,
For every gift your goodness sends,
   We thank You, gracious Lord.

*Anonymous*

## A Child's Morning Prayer

Praised be Thou, O Lord our God, Father of all,
   for letting me see this new day.
O God, guard my tongue from evil,
   and my lips from speaking falsehood.
O Lord, help me to understand Thy teachings,
   and to be faithful to all my duties.
Let my prayer be acceptable in Thy sight, O Lord.
Amen.

*from "The Jewish Woman and Her Home"*
*by Hyman E. Goldin*

O Lord, You know how busy
I must be today.
If I forget You,
do not forget me.

*Jacob Astley*

## The Prayer of the Little Bird

Dear God,
I don't know how to pray by myself
very well,
but will You please
protect my little nest from wind and rain?
Put a great deal of dew on the flowers,
many seeds in my way.

Make Your blue very high,
Your branches lissom;
let Your kind light stay late in the sky
and set my heart brimming with such music
that I must sing, sing, sing . . . .
Please, Lord.

                                        Amen.

Carmen Bernos de Gasztold
(translated by Rumer Godden)

## The Prayer of the Mouse

I am so little and gray,
dear God,
how can You keep me in mind?
Always spied upon,
always chased.
Nobody ever gives me anything,
and I nibble meagerly at life.
Why do they reproach me with being a mouse?
Who made me but You?
I only ask to stay hidden.
Give me my hunger's pittance
safe from the claws
of that devil with green eyes.

                        Amen.

Carmen Bernos de Gasztold
(translated by Rumer Godden)

# The Prayer of the Little Ducks

Dear God,
give us a flood of water.
Let it rain tomorrow and always.
Give us plenty of little slugs
and other luscious things to eat.
Protect all folk who quack
and everyone who knows how to swim.

Amen.

Carmen Bernos de Gasztold
(translated by Rumer Godden)

"If I am not for myself, who will be for me?
And if I am only for myself, what am I?
And if not now, when?"

The Talmud

In dealing with others,
know how to be gentle and kind.

Lao Tsu,
The Tao Cheh Ching

If we have ever been mean to one who loves us,
ever wronged a friend or playmate,
the child next door or a stranger,
O Lord, take away our sin.

If we have ever cheated at our games,
not meaning to or on purpose,
take away our sin, O Lord,
and let us be your own beloved children.

The Rig Veda (adapted)

Sing praise to the Lord!
Sing praise!

Psalm 47:6

God of the winds and waters, of fire and death!
Lord of the solitary moon, the Creator,
                    the Ancestor of all!
Adoration unto Thee, a thousand adorations;
    and again and again unto Thee adoration.

The Bhagavad Gita
(translated by Juan Mascaro)

## A Little Girl Prays

Dear God,
My Dad says
  You want me
  to love You
  more than
  I love him . . . .
  or Mommy.
I wondered
  how I could.
I asked my Dad
  about it
  and he said:
"Well, you love
  the cookies
  Mommy makes
  and gives you.
And you love Mommy
  more than
  you love
  the cookies.
It is something
  like that.
You love
  your Mommy and Dad,
  and your Mommy and Dad
  love you.
God gave us to you,
  and He gave
  you to us.
God gives us
  all good things.
God loves us.
That is why
  we love Him
  with all our heart,
  with all our soul,
  with all our strength."
That is what my Dad said.
I do love You, God,
  and thank You. Amen.

*E. W.*

*The Snail does the Holy*
*Will of God slowly.*

G. K. Chesterton

Dear God,
My Mommy is always
    telling me to hurry.
It takes me
    a long time
    to put on my socks,
    she says;
And a long time
    to tie my
    shoelaces.
I tell her
    no matter what
    I'm doing
    I like to
    think about things.
She hugs me
    and calls me
    her little Snail.
He does Your holy
    will slowly,
    she says.
She wants me
    to do Your will, too,
    but a little bit
    faster
    because I'm a boy.
I'll try, dear God. Amen.

E. W.

15

When someone is wronged, he must put aside all resentment and say,
   "My mind shall not be disturbed;
   no angry word shall escape my lips;
   I will remain kind and friendly,
   with loving thoughts
   and no secret spite."

*A Buddhist Prayer*


O Lord, keep me from trampling
   the tender feelings of friends,
   whether at school or at play. Amen.

*E. W.*

As the fire under the stone floor
    of my dwelling place
        burns brightly to warm my house,
So may the love of God
    warm my heart
        and the hearts of those
    who step over my threshold.

A Formosan Prayer

By this shall all men know that we are his disciples,
    if we have love for one another.

John 13:35

## A Child's Prayer

There's no one awake
  in the world but me
And the robin singing
  in the apple tree.

God bless the robin
And God bless me.

God bless my eyes
And the things I see,
A big blue flower
And a bumble bee.

God bless my ears
And the sounds I hear,
The rustle of leaves
  in the poplar trees
  far and near.

And bless my feet
Wherever I go
  running fast,
  walking slow.

God bless the words
I say today.
Let them be kind
  and friendly.

Bless the people
    that I meet
As I go riding
    down the street
On my bike
    that I like.

God bless our house:
    Its bright red door,
    Its window eyes,
    Its chimney soaring
    to the skies.

God bless all who live here.
God bless all we do here.
God bless everything.

                    E. W.

# The Golden Rule

You must love your neighbor as yourself.

Romans 13:9

Do to no one what you would not want
done to you.

Tobit 4:15

He sought for others the good
he desired for himself. Let him pass.

The Egyptian Book of the Dead

So always treat others as you would
like them to treat you.

Matthew 7:12, Luke 6:31

What you would not want done to yourself,
do not to others.

Confucius (Chinese sage)

One should seek for others
the happiness one desires for himself.

The Buddha (Indian philosopher)

In your dealings with others, harm not
that you be not harmed.

Seneca (a Roman)

The true rule of life is to guard
and to do by the things of others
as one would to his own.

Hindu Scripture

We should behave toward friends
as we would wish friends to behave
toward us.

Aristotle (Greek philosopher)

## A Japanese Prayer

Oh, make my heart so still, so still,
When I am deep in prayer,
That I might hear the white-mist-wreaths
Losing themselves in air.

## A Jewish Prayer

Remember us for life,
King who delights in life,
And inscribe us
In the Book of Life
For Your sake,
God of life.

## A Christian Prayer

God be in my head
  And in my understanding;
God be in my eyes,
  And in my looking;
God be in my mouth,
  And in my speaking;
God be in my heart,
  And in my thinking;
God be at my end,
  And at my departing.

*The Sarum Primer*

## A Muslim Prayer

I confess there is no God but God,
  I confess there is no God but God.

Someone's loving, Lord.

Someone's praying, Lord.

Someone's giving, Lord.

# Kumbaya

Author Unknown

Some — one's sing — ing, Lord, kum — ba — ya; Some — one's sing — ing, Lord, kum — ba — ya;

Some — one's sing — ing, Lord, kum — ba — ya; O Lord, kum — ba — ya.

Someone's hungry, Lord.

Someone's **happy**, Lord.

Someone's praising, Lord.

# Bless the Lord

All you things the Lord has made, bless the Lord;
  Give Him glory and praise forever!

Sun and moon, bless the Lord;
  Bless the Lord, you stars of heaven.

Dew and rain, bless the Lord;
  Bless the Lord, you winds.

Frost and cold, bless the Lord;
  Bless the Lord, you ice and snow.

Springs of water, bless the Lord;
  Bless the Lord, you seas and rivers.

Fire and heat, bless the Lord;
  Bless the Lord, all things that grow.

Birds of heaven, bless the Lord;
  Bless the Lord, you animals wild and tame.

All you people, bless the Lord;
  Bless the Lord, you children.

Give glory to the Lord!
  Praise Him forever! Alleluia!

*The Book of Daniel (adapted)*

## Grace for a Child

Here a little child I stand,
Heaving up my either hand;
Cold as paddocks though they be,
Here I lift them up to Thee,
For a benison to fall
On our meat and on us all. Amen.

*Robert Herrick*

Blessed art Thou,
    O Lord, our King,
Who feedest every
    Living thing;

Who givest bread,
    So that we may
Have strength to do
    Our work each day;

Blessed art Thou,
    For Thou dost give
Food to nourish
    All that live.

*Ilo Orleans*

*Kindly words are a honeycomb,*
*sweetness to the soul*
*and health to the body.*

*Proverbs 16:24*

What God gives
   and what we take
'Tis a gift for Christ,
   His sake;
Be the meal
   of beans or peas,
God be thanked
   for those and these;
Have we flesh,
   or have we fish,
All are fragments
   from His dish.

*Robert Herrick*

O Lord,
by this meal You bring us together
in joy and peace.
Keep us always united in Your love
through Christ our Lord. Amen.

*M. D. Bouyer*

Dear God, I gratefully
   bow my head
To thank You
   for this daily bread;
And may there be
   a goodly share
On every table
   everywhere. Amen.

*Dixie Willson*

## Prayer of a Contented Boy

St. Paul said, "I have learned in whatsoever state I am to be contented therewith."

I think I've found the way, O Lord,
　Always contented to be:
To like and to see Your will, O Lord,
　In whatever happens to me.

　　　　　　　　　　E. W.

Be bold as a leopard, and swift as an eagle, and fleet as a hart, and strong as a lion

to do the will of thy Father who is in Heaven.

The Talmud

## Prayer for the Burial of a Bird

This sparrow died today, O Lord,
Your feathered creature small.
We lay him in the friendly earth
And ask Your blessing on us all.

E. W.

There are three ways children express sorrow:
  Some children cry;
  Some children are silent;
  Wise children know how to turn sorrow
    into song.        Hassidic Writings (adapted)

## Little Things

Little things that run and quail
  And die in silence and despair;

Little things that fight and fail
  And fall on sea and earth and air;

All trapped and frightened little things,
  The mouse, the coney, hear our prayer:

As we forgive those done to us,
  The lamb, the linnet, and the hare,

Forgive us all our trespasses,
  Little creatures everywhere.

*James Stephens*


Dear Father, hear and bless
Thy beasts and singing birds,
And guard with tenderness
Small things that have no words.

*Anonymous*


He prayeth best who loveth best
All things both great and small,
For the dear God who loveth us
He made and loveth all.

*Samuel Taylor Coleridge*

## An American Indian Prayer

O Great Spirit,
Whose voice I hear in the winds,
And whose breath gives life to all the world,
Hear me! I am small and weak, I need your
Strength and wisdom.

Let Me Walk In Beauty, and make my eyes
ever behold the red and purple sunset.

Make My Hands respect the things you have
made and my ears sharp to hear your voice.

Make Me Wise so that I may understand the
things you have taught my people.

Let Me Learn the Lessons you have hidden in
every leaf and rock.

I Seek Strength, not to be greater than my
brother, but to fight my greatest enemy—myself.

Make Me Always Ready to come to you with clean
hands and straight eyes.

So When Life Fades, as the fading sunset, my
spirit may come to you without shame.

## Heaven

Heaven is
The place where
Happiness is
Everywhere.
Animals
And birds sing—
As does
Everything.
To each stone,
"How-do-you-do?"
"Well!! And you?"

Langston Hughes

*Talking with one another
is loving one another.*

African

## Shema
## "The Lord is One"

Hear, Israel:
The Lord is our God.
The Lord is One.

Blessed be his name
Whose glorious kingdom
Is for ever and ever.
And you shall love
The Lord your God
With all your soul
And with all your might.
And these words
Which I command you this day
Shall be upon your heart.
And you shall teach them diligently
To your children,
And shall talk of them
When you sit in your house,
And when you walk on the way,
And when you lie down,
And when you rise up.
And you shall bind them
For a sign on your hand,
And they shall be for frontlets
Between your eyes;
And you shall write them
On the doorposts of your house
And on your gates.

*translated by Bernard Martin*

Praise be to God, Lord of the worlds!
The compassionate, the merciful!
King on the day of reckoning!
Thee only do we worship,
    and to Thee do we cry for help.
Guide Thou us on the straight path,
The path of those to whom
    Thou hast been gracious,
    with whom Thou art not angry
    and who do not go astray. Amen.

The Koran

God is greatest, God is greatest,
    God is greatest, God is greatest.

*Muslim prayer that is
whispered into a newborn baby's ears*

# An Irish Hymn

Praise and gratitude to you, Holy Father,
Who created the skies and heaven first
And after that created the big wet sea
And the heaps of fish in it swimming closely.

*An ancient hymn from the Great Blasket Island*

# Prayer of the Breton Fisherman

Dear God,
Be good to me.
The sea is so wide
And my boat is so small.

# To You, O Lord, I Lift up My Hands in Prayer

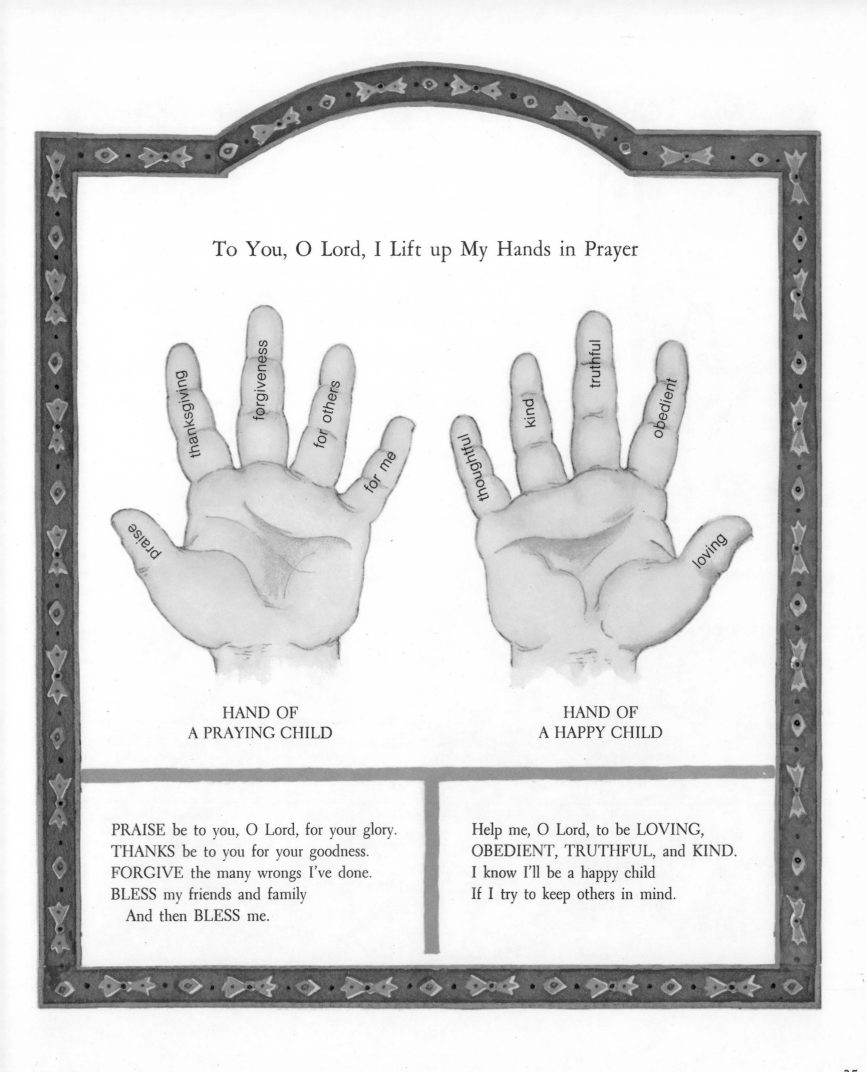

HAND OF
A PRAYING CHILD

HAND OF
A HAPPY CHILD

PRAISE be to you, O Lord, for your glory.
THANKS be to you for your goodness.
FORGIVE the many wrongs I've done.
BLESS my friends and family
    And then BLESS me.

Help me, O Lord, to be LOVING,
OBEDIENT, TRUTHFUL, and KIND.
I know I'll be a happy child
If I try to keep others in mind.

## Song of the Sun

O most high almighty, good Lord God, to Thee belong praise, glory, honor, and all blessing!

Praised be my Lord God with all His creatures; and especially our brother the sun, who brings us the day, and who brings us the light; fair is he, and shining with a very great splendor.

Praised be my Lord for our sister the moon, and for the stars the which He has set clear and lovely in heaven.

Praised be my Lord for our sister water, who is very serviceable unto us, and humble, and precious, and clean.

Praised be my mother the earth, the which doth sustain us and keep us, and bringeth forth divers fruits, and flowers of many colors, and grass.

Praise ye, and bless ye the Lord, and give thanks unto Him and serve Him with great humility.

*St. Francis of Assisi*
*(translated by Matthew Arnold)*

# The Prayer of the Cricket

O God,
I am little and very black
but I thank You
for having shed
Your warm sun
and the quivering of Your golden corn
on my humble life.
Then take—but be forebearing, Lord—
this little impulse of my love,
this note of music
You have set thrilling in my heart.

Carmen Bernos de Gasztold
(translated by Rumer Godden)

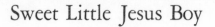

## Sweet Little Jesus Boy

Sweet little Jesus boy
Born long time ago
Sweet little Holy Child
And we didn't know who you were.
We didn't know you came to save us, Lord.
To take our sins away. . . .
You taught us how,
We're trying.
Master, you showed us how
Even when you were dying.

*A Spiritual*

38

## What Child Is This?

What child is this, who, laid to rest,
On Mary's lap is sleeping?
Whom angels greet with anthems sweet,
While shepherds watch are keeping?

REFRAIN

This, this is Christ the King,
Whom shepherds guard and angels sing:
Haste, haste to bring him laud,
The babe, the son of Mary.

Why lies he in such mean estate
Where ox and ass are feeding?
Good Christian, fear; for sinners here
The silent Word is pleading.

REFRAIN

So bring him incense, gold, and myrrh,
Come, peasant, king, to own him,
The King of kings salvation brings,
Let loving hearts enthrone him.

REFRAIN                    William C. Dix
                          (sung to "Greensleeves")

Jesus Christ, Thou Child so wise,
Bless mine hands and fill mine eyes,
And bring my soul to Paradise.

Hilaire Belloc

## A Prayer for Hanukkah

O Lord God, be with us and with our children today.
Imbue us with perfect faith in Thee.
Make us strong to do Thy will.
Bless the Hanukkah lights that they may shed their
    radiance into our homes and our lives.
May they kindle within us the flame of faith and zeal
    so that we may battle bravely for Thy cause.
Make us worthy of Thy love and Thy blessing.
Let injustice and oppression cease,
    and cruelty, hatred and wrong pass away,
    so that all men may unite
    to worship Thy holy name. Amen.

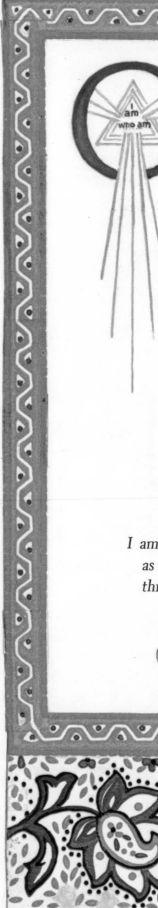

# The Lord's Prayer

Our Father in heaven,
holy be your Name,
your kingdom come,
your will be done,
    on earth as it is in heaven.
Give us today our daily bread.
Forgive us our sins
    as we forgive those who sin against us.
Do not bring us to the test
    but deliver us from evil.

For the kingdom, the power, and the glory
    are yours now and forever.

*Used in Service for Unity*

*I am in every religion*
    *as a thread*
        *through a string of pearls.*

*Hindu*

41

# A Child's Evening Prayer

Praised be Thou, O Lord our God, Father of all,
  for giving us the sweet rest of the night.
In peace do I lay me down to sleep,
  and may it be Thy will, O Lord,
  that I awake in peace.
I am in the care of the Lord
  when I sleep and when I wake.
In Thy help I trust, O Lord.

*from "The Jewish Woman and Her Home"*
*by Hyman E. Goldin*

Matthew, Mark, Luke, and John,
Bless the bed that I lie on.
  Four corners to my bed,
  Four angels round my head;
  One to watch and one to pray,
  And two to bear my soul away.

*Traditional*

# Jesus, Tender Shepherd, Hear Me

Jesus, tender Shepherd, hear me;
Bless Thy little lamb tonight;
Through the darkness be Thou near me,
Watch my sleep till morning light.

All this day Thy hand has led me,
And I thank Thee for Thy care;
Thou has warmed and clothed and fed me;
Listen to my evening prayer.

Mary L. Duncan

This I know in heaven above,
All hope and joy are there.
In the circle of His love,
There's room for all—
And to spare.

*A Spiritual*

# NOTES

Page 9.  Jacob Astley, who took part in the civil war that Englishmen fought against their king, Charles I, said this prayer before the battle of Edgehill on October 23, 1642.

Page 12.  The Chinese *Tao Cheh Ching* is a collection of poems and sayings of Lao Tsu, who was born in 604 B.C. His teachings became known as *Taoism*, a name taken from the word *Tao*, which means *a way* or *a road*.

The *Rig Veda*, the most important of the four Hindu Vedas, is a collection of prayers and praises dating from about 1500 B.C.

Page 13.  The *Bhagavad Gita*, from the year 1 A.D., is the book most respected by Hindus. It is a long philosophical poem.

Page 16.  Buddhism has been the religion of millions of Asians for over 2500 years. Its great teacher was born in 563 B.C. and was known as the Buddha.

Page 21.  The *Sarum Primer*, dating from 1558 A.D., was a collection of devotional prayers and hymns used by priests and people in the English Church.

This Muslim Prayer is said by the *muezzin*, who calls Muslims to prayer five times a day. He begins by saying "God is greatest" four times. Then he repeats twice "I confess there is no God but God."

Page 22.  *Kumbaya* is an African word that means *be with us*.

Page 24.  Paddocks are toads or frogs.
A *benison* is a blessing.

Page 26.  Some Jewish laws, handed down by word of mouth for hundreds of years, were called the *Mishna*. Every point of them was studied in great detail by Jewish scholars, whose comments were known as the *Gemara*. Then, about 1500 years ago, both the *Mishna* and the *Gemara* were written down in what we know today as the Talmud.

Page 27.  The *Hassidim* are members of a sect of pious Jews, founded in 1750 in Poland. For the true Hassid, all of God's creation is filled with music and beauty, and he expresses his joy in this beauty in singing and dancing and in his writings.

Page 32.  *Shema* means *hear*. This prayer is found in Deuteronomy 6:4-9, and was said every day in the Temple in Jerusalem. It is now part of the synagogue service. When saying it as a morning prayer, men bind leather straps, containing boxes that hold Bible verses, around the left arm ("For a sign on your hand") and around the head ("And they shall be for frontlets between your eyes").

Page 33.  The religion we know as *Islam* was founded in Arabia by Muhammed, who was born in 570 A.D. Its holy book, the *Koran*, gives the religious duties, teachings, and prayers of the members of Islam, who are known as *Muslims*.

Page 40.  Hanukkah, or the Feast of Lights, is a happy holiday that comes in November or December. On this day, the Jewish people remember the defeat of the Syrians by the hero, Judas Maccabeus. On that day, too, they remember the rekindling of the light in the Temple.

Page 42.  Many versions of the "Matthew, Mark, Luke, and John" prayer can be found in Europe. A Latin version, set down in 1532, is sung in the opera, *Hansel and Gretel*, written in 1893. The prayer is known in such northern lands as Norway and Sweden, and in Spain and France in southern Europe.

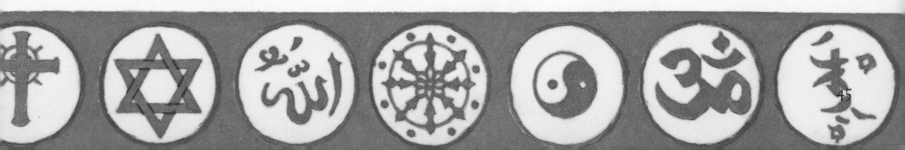